# 7 Landmark Cases That Changed The Indian Judicial System

**NARAYANA SWAMY .R**

Advocate Karnataka

# Acknowledgements and Dedication

This book is lovingly dedicated to the memories and unwavering support of my family, who have been my greatest sources of strength and inspiration.

To my late father, **Rangappa M.K.**, and my mother, **Lakshminarasamma** your values and guidance have been the foundation of my life and work. This book is a tribute to the resilience, wisdom, and integrity you instilled in me.

To my brother, **Shivashankara** thank you for always standing by my side, offering encouragement and support in countless ways. Your belief in me has meant more than words can express.

And to my beloved wife, **Gowthami M.N** your patience, love, and encouragement have been my anchor through every step of this journey. This book would not have been possible without your strength and unwavering support.

With heartfelt gratitude, I dedicate this work to each of you.

# Preface

In a country as vast and diverse as India, the judiciary serves as a beacon of justice, constantly navigating the evolving social landscape to uphold the principles enshrined in the Constitution. With a population of over a billion, each judgment rendered by the courts can have wide-reaching effects, shaping laws, policies, and societal norms. 7 Landmark Cases That Changed the Indian Judicial System seeks to illuminate the stories and legal principles behind some of the most influential judgments in India's history. Each of these cases represents a defining moment, where the judiciary not only interpreted the law but also transformed it, pushing the boundaries of justice to protect individual rights and promote a more equitable society.

This book dives into seven pivotal cases, unpacking each one through a comprehensive analysis. From the courage of individuals like Mary Roy, who fought for equal inheritance rights, to the tragic yet transformative Nirbhaya case that changed the landscape of laws on sexual violence, each chapter brings to life the backgrounds, arguments, and impacts of these landmark decisions. For legal professionals, students, and laypeople alike, this book provides both a foundational understanding of each case and a deeper insight into how the judiciary has navigated complex issues with far-reaching implications.

A unique feature of this book is its provision of Direct Access to Citations. Each case study includes a **QR code** that enables readers to instantly access and download primary sources, legal authorities, and citations referenced in the analysis. This feature makes legal research both efficient and convenient, allowing readers to verify and explore the sources behind each judgment without the typical time-consuming search. This **QR code** system, meticulously curated for each case, supports the book's aim of being a reliable resource for anyone interested in delving deeper into these landmark judgments, whether for academic purposes, professional reference, or personal interest.

In writing 7 Landmark Cases That Changed the Indian Judicial System, I sought to create a book that celebrates the resilience of those who challenged the status quo and the power of the judiciary to bring about meaningful change. It is my hope that readers will find inspiration not only in the stories of those who sought justice but also in the ability of the judiciary to respond to society's evolving needs with wisdom, courage, and a deep sense of duty.

This book is not just a collection of legal analyses but a tribute to the spirit of the Indian judiciary, which continues to protect the rights and freedoms of its citizens. As you turn these pages, may you gain a renewed appreciation for the impact of the law on everyday life and be inspired by the cases that have shaped the journey of justice in India.

**NARAYANASWAMY.R**

**Advocate, Karnataka**

# TABLE OF CONTENTS

# CHAPTER-1

## THE NIRBHAYA CASE: A TURNING POINT IN INDIA'S CRIMINAL JUSTICE SYSTEM

## Introduction and Background of the Case

Few cases have shaken a nation's conscience as profoundly as the Nirbhaya Case, officially titled Mukesh & Anr. vs. State for NCT of Delhi & Ors. This case became a flashpoint in India's struggle against sexual violence, sparking waves of protests and an outpouring of national grief. The brutal gang rape and murder of a 23-year-old physiotherapy intern on the night of December 16, 2012, in New Delhi led to unprecedented demands for justice and systemic reforms. The intensity of public outrage forced both the judiciary and the government to confront the gaps in India's legal approach to crimes against women, catalyzing a series of reforms that reshaped Indian criminal law.

Nirbhaya, as the victim was later known, had boarded a private bus with her male friend, hoping to reach home safely. However, the bus was driven by a group of six men, including a 17-year-old juvenile, who turned their journey into a nightmare. They tortured and raped her over several hours, using an iron rod that caused grievous injuries, leading to her multi-organ failure. The perpetrators then discarded her and her friend from the moving bus, leaving her critically injured on the roadside. Despite extensive medical efforts in India and Singapore, she succumbed to her injuries on December 29, 2012.

## Facts of the Case

The facts of this case highlight both the brutality of the crime and the urgency of reform:

- The Attack: Nirbhaya and her friend boarded the private bus, unaware of the group's intentions. The six men gang-raped and beat her, using a rod that caused irreversible damage, eventually throwing both victims out of the bus.

- Medical Efforts and National Reaction: Despite medical intervention, her injuries were so severe that she passed away after nearly two weeks, sparking nationwide protests that called for justice and the reformation of sexual assault laws.

- Apprehension and Sentencing: The six men were quickly arrested, and a trial ensued. Of the accused, one was a juvenile, receiving a lighter sentence due to his age, which generated public outrage and calls to amend juvenile justice laws.

## Issues Raised

The Nirbhaya case raised several critical issues:

1. Legal Definitions and Scope: Did existing laws on sexual violence adequately cover the various forms of brutality suffered by the victim?

2. Juvenile Justice: Should the age threshold for juveniles be reconsidered in cases involving heinous crimes?

3. Efficiency of Legal Processes: Could the judiciary ensure swift justice for victims of brutal crimes?

4. Accountability of Public Safety Institutions: What role should the state play in ensuring women's safety?

## Laws Discussed

Several key legal provisions and doctrines came under scrutiny:

- Indian Penal Code (IPC): The case exposed the limitations of the IPC's definitions of sexual violence, which had not kept pace with contemporary needs.

- Juvenile Justice Act: The lenient treatment of the 17-year-old involved in the crime triggered demands for reform, leading to amendments that lowered the age of adult responsibility to 16 in cases of heinous offenses.

- "Rarest of Rare" Doctrine: The Court emphasized this doctrine, which reserves capital punishment for cases where the crime's brutality defies humanity.

## Arguments of the Parties

- Prosecution's Argument: The prosecution argued for the death penalty for the four adult convicts, invoking the "rarest of rare" doctrine to emphasize that the brutality of the crime merited capital punishment. The prosecution contended that the perpetrators' cruelty necessitated a strict punishment to deter future crimes of this nature.

- Defense's Argument: The defense argued for a reduction in sentences, citing potential rehabilitation. However, given the overwhelming evidence and the public sentiment, these arguments were met with limited consideration by the Court.

## Judgment of the Case

The trial moved swiftly through the Indian judicial system, reflecting the demand for prompt justice. The trial court sentenced the four adult convicts to death, a decision subsequently upheld by both the Delhi High Court and the Supreme Court. The Court invoked the "rarest of rare" doctrine, underscoring that the crime's inhumanity justified the ultimate penalty. The juvenile was sentenced to a three-year term in a correctional facility, in accordance with the Juvenile Justice Act at the time, which led to a national debate on juvenile culpability.

## Analysis of the Judgment

The Supreme Court's decision balanced retribution with deterrence, emphasizing that the judiciary would not tolerate crimes of such brutality. The judgment resonated deeply, signaling a shift in the judiciary's approach toward sexual violence cases. The Court recognized that societal attitudes needed to evolve alongside legal protections, and it emphasized the importance of deterrent sentencing. However, the juvenile's lenient sentence led to significant public debate, which ultimately influenced amendments in juvenile law to ensure that young offenders committing heinous crimes could be tried as adults.

## Impact of the Judgment

The Nirbhaya judgment spurred significant legal reforms:

1. Criminal Law (Amendment) Act, 2013: This Act expanded the definition of rape, introduced stringent penalties for various forms of sexual violence, and established fast-track courts for such cases.

2. Amendment to the Juvenile Justice Act, 2015: The Act was amended to allow juveniles aged 16 to 18 to be tried as adults in cases involving heinous crimes, reflecting the national sentiment that age should not excuse the severity of punishment for brutal offenses.

3. Justice Verma Committee: The government appointed the Justice J.S. Verma Committee to recommend broader legal reforms to protect women. The Committee's report led to several changes, including the criminalization of voyeurism, stalking, and acid attacks, and enhanced victim support.

## Conclusion

The Nirbhaya Case marked a watershed moment in India's fight for women's safety and justice. This case galvanized a nation, prompting comprehensive legal reforms that reshaped India's approach to gender-based violence. The case underscored the need for a robust legal system capable of both punishing and deterring such heinous acts, while also addressing gaps in juvenile justice. Today, the Nirbhaya Case stands as a powerful symbol of resilience and justice, reminding us of the need for continued vigilance and reform to protect women's rights in India. It remains a testament to the nation's commitment to creating a society where justice is not only swift but also transformative.

*Scan Me to Download*

# CHAPTER-2

# SHAH BANO CASE: WOMEN'S RIGHTS AND SECULARISM

## Introduction to the Case

The Mohd. Ahmed Khan v. Shah Bano Begum case, decided on April 23, 1985, is one of the landmark rulings by the Supreme Court of India, widely regarded as a pivotal moment in the interplay between personal law and the Indian Constitution. This case, involving the rights of a divorced Muslim woman to claim maintenance under Section 125 of the Code of Criminal Procedure (CrPC), transcended individual circumstances and raised far-reaching questions about secularism, social justice, and the concept of equality before the law. The case, and the ensuing judicial and social discourse, not only addressed the rights of divorced Muslim women but also underscored the necessity of a Uniform Civil Code, a long-debated provision of the Indian Constitution.

## Background of the Case

The case originated when Shah Bano Begum, a 62-year-old woman, was divorced by her husband, Mohd. Ahmed Khan, through talaq. Driven out of her matrimonial home, she approached the court, claiming maintenance under Section 125 of the CrPC. This provision mandates that any individual with sufficient means must support their spouse if they are unable to maintain themselves, irrespective of religion. Khan contended that, under Muslim Personal Law, his obligation ended after providing maintenance during the iddat period, or three months post-divorce.

## Facts of the Case

Shah Bano, married in 1932, was financially dependent on her husband. After 43 years of marriage, Khan unilaterally divorced her in 1978, offering only a minimal Mahr (dower) and maintenance for the short iddat period. Arguing that this provision was inadequate, Shah Bano sought a monthly allowance under CrPC provisions. The Judicial Magistrate initially ordered Khan to pay a nominal amount, later revised to Rs. 179.20 per month by the Madhya Pradesh High Court. Dissatisfied, Khan appealed to the Supreme Court, arguing that, according to Muslim Personal Law, he had no further obligation beyond the iddat period.

## Issues Raised

1. Does Section 125 of the CrPC apply to Muslims, potentially conflicting with personal law?

2. Is a divorced Muslim woman entitled to claim maintenance under this provision, even after the iddat period?

3. Does payment of Mahr (dowry) and maintenance during the iddat period suffice as final settlement?

## Laws Discussed

The Supreme Court focused on Sections 125 and 127 of the CrPC, which establish maintenance provisions irrespective of religious affiliations, aiming to prevent destitution and vagrancy. The judgment also examined Muslim Personal Law regarding the responsibilities of husbands to provide financial support post-divorce and the Islamic concept of Mahr.

## Arguments of the Parties

- Petitioner (Khan): Khan argued that Muslim Personal Law limited his financial obligation to Shah Bano to the iddat period and the sum of Mahr. He claimed that Section 125 should not interfere with these religious customs.

- Respondent (Shah Bano): Shah Bano contended that Section 125 CrPC was secular and applied to all Indian citizens, including Muslims. She argued that financial support beyond iddat was essential for her survival, and denying it would violate her fundamental rights.

## Judgment of the Case

The Supreme Court, led by Chief Justice Y.V. Chandrachud, ruled in favor of Shah Bano, upholding her right to maintenance under Section 125 CrPC. The Court affirmed that personal laws cannot supersede a citizen's right to financial security, declaring that Section 125 applied to all citizens equally. Additionally, it emphasized that Muslim husbands have an obligation to ensure their ex-wives' financial well-being, invoking the principles of the Quran to underline this duty.

## Analysis of the Judgment

The judgment showcased the Supreme Court's commitment to justice, especially for vulnerable sections of society. While respecting personal laws, the Court highlighted the secular and humanitarian intent of Section 125, emphasizing that maintenance rights extended beyond religious boundaries. This ruling thus reinforced the principle that all citizens, irrespective of religion, are entitled to basic legal protections under Indian law.

## Significance and Aftermath

The Shah Bano judgment was celebrated by advocates of secularism and women's rights, as it underscored the need for a Uniform Civil Code to ensure equality and justice. However, the ruling also sparked substantial backlash from conservative factions within the Muslim community, who perceived it as a violation of religious freedoms. In response, the Indian government passed the Muslim Women (Protection of Rights on Divorce) Act, 1986, aiming to limit divorced Muslim women's maintenance rights to the iddat period, thereby diluting the impact of the Shah Bano decision.

## Conclusion

The Shah Bano case remains a seminal moment in Indian legal history, illustrating the judiciary's role in balancing personal laws with constitutional guarantees. While the political response to the judgment was polarizing, it catalyzed discussions on women's rights, religious freedom, and legal uniformity in India. The case continues to inspire debate on the intersection of secular law and religious customs, reflecting an ongoing struggle to create an inclusive and equitable society for all Indian citizens.

*Scan Me to Download*

# CHAPTER-3

# MATHURA RAPE CASE: A CATALYST FOR RAPE LAW REFORM IN INDIA

## Introduction

The Mathura Rape Case of 1972, also known as Tuka Ram &
Anr. vs. State of Maharashtra, is one of the most controversial
and consequential legal battles in Indian history. This case
involved the custodial rape of a young tribal girl, Mathura, by two
policemen and ultimately led to their acquittal by the Supreme
Court. The Court's decision in this case, which questioned the
concept of consent and allowed the accused to go unpunished,
ignited nationwide outrage and highlighted glaring gaps in the
Indian legal system's approach to sexual violence. The public
outcry over this verdict led to widespread protests and significant
amendments to India's rape laws, aiming to strengthen
protections for women and clarify legal standards of consent.

## Background of the Case

Mathura was a 16-year-old tribal girl living in Maharashtra who
became entangled in a police investigation due to a family dispute.
On the night of March 26, 1972, she was summoned to the Desai
Ganj Police Station, where she was questioned along with her
family members. After the initial questioning ended around 10:30
p.m., Mathura and her family prepared to leave. However, two
policemen, Head Constable Tukaram and Constable Ganpat,
ordered Mathura to remain while asking her family to leave the
station.

Once alone with Mathura, Ganpat led her to a secluded area
within the police station and raped her. Tukaram, the head

constable, also attempted to assault her but failed due to intoxication. When Mathura emerged from the police station, she immediately informed her family of the assault. A medical examination later revealed semen stains on her clothing, but no physical injuries or evidence of struggle, as Mathura was described as "habituated to sexual intercourse."

## Facts of the Case

The primary facts that emerged during the trial were:

- Mathura's initial lack of physical resistance was cited as an indication of "passive submission," leading the lower court to question whether her actions implied consent.

- The medical examination showed no injuries on Mathura's body, a fact that was misinterpreted as lack of resistance and thus, consent.

- Mathura's young age, social vulnerability, and the unequal power dynamic between her and the policemen were largely overlooked by the courts.

## Issues Raised

1. Consent and Passive Submission: The central issue was whether Mathura's lack of overt physical resistance constituted consent, with the court failing to account for the power imbalance and psychological trauma associated with custodial rape.

2. Onus of Proving Non-Consent: The case raised questions about the burden of proof in rape cases and the responsibility of the prosecution to demonstrate that the act was against the victim's will.

3. Judicial Understanding of Custodial Rape: The case highlighted the lack of legal provisions specifically addressing rape in custodial situations and the systemic bias against marginalized women.

## Laws Discussed

The key law discussed was Section 375 of the Indian Penal Code, which defined rape and included clauses that addressed situations where consent was obtained through fear of death or hurt. The Court's interpretation of this section, however, was limited, focusing narrowly on physical resistance and ignoring the context of coercion in custodial situations.

## Arguments of the Parties

- Prosecution's Argument: The prosecution argued that Mathura did not consent to the act and that her inability to physically resist was a result of intimidation and fear, not willingness. They contended that the power dynamics and circumstances invalidated any argument of consent.

- Defense's Argument: The defense argued that Mathura had shown "passive submission," and her lack of visible injuries indicated consent. They claimed that no coercion or fear of harm was demonstrated, and thus, the act could not legally qualify as rape.

## Judgment of the Case

In 1978, the Supreme Court acquitted the two policemen, citing that Mathura had not shown sufficient signs of physical resistance, and that her "passive submission" could not be equated with non-consent. The Court relied on the absence of injuries to conclude that the act was consensual. This judgment was widely criticized for its failure to consider the custodial setting and the psychological coercion involved, effectively allowing the perpetrators to evade accountability.

## Analysis of the Judgment

The judgment exposed profound flaws in the Indian judiciary's understanding of sexual consent, especially in custodial situations where victims are likely to feel powerless to resist. By equating lack of physical struggle with consent, the Court ignored the fear, intimidation, and power imbalance that custodial rape victims face. This interpretation neglected the psychological coercion inherent in a custodial setting, setting a dangerous precedent that placed undue emphasis on physical resistance.

## Impact of the Judgment

The Supreme Court's ruling sparked a wave of public outrage, with activists, academics, and women's organizations across India condemning the verdict. An open letter to the Chief Justice, penned by renowned lawyers and academics, argued that the judgment perpetuated injustice and failed to protect women, especially marginalized women, from sexual violence. The nationwide protests led to the Criminal Law (Amendment) Act of 1983, which introduced several key reforms:

- Recognition of Custodial Rape: The amended law included specific provisions for custodial rape, acknowledging that sexual assault within police custody involved coercion and was distinct from other forms of sexual violence.

- Shift in Burden of Proof: The law shifted the burden of proof in cases of custodial rape, requiring the accused to demonstrate that the act was consensual rather than placing the onus entirely on the survivor.

- Expanded Definition of Consent: The amendment clarified that lack of physical resistance does not imply consent, setting a new legal standard for understanding consent.

## Conclusion

The Mathura Rape Case stands as a crucial turning point in India's criminal justice system, prompting legal reforms that have strengthened protections for survivors of sexual violence. It exposed the need for judicial sensitivity in cases of custodial rape, recognizing that power imbalances and psychological coercion are vital elements in assessing consent. The outrage surrounding this case and the subsequent legal reforms underscore the importance of a judiciary that upholds justice over technicalities and empowers marginalized communities. Today, the Mathura Case is remembered as a dark moment that catalyzed vital changes, ensuring that future victims of custodial violence would have a more supportive and just legal framework.

*Scan Me to Download*

CHAPTER-4


# KM NANAVATI VS. STATE OF MAHARASHTRA: THE TRIAL THAT SHAPED INDIA'S JUDICIAL SYSTEM

## Introduction

The KM Nanavati vs. State of Maharashtra case, decided in 1959, remains one of the most infamous and transformative legal battles in Indian history. This high-profile murder trial, centered around themes of betrayal, honor, and crime, gripped the nation and ultimately led to the abolition of India's jury system. Through its sensational details and the influence of public opinion, the case revealed the challenges of maintaining impartiality in jury trials and set the stage for substantial judicial reforms, transforming India's approach to criminal justice.

## Background of the Case

Commander Kawas Manekshaw Nanavati was a respected naval officer, married to Sylvia, with whom he shared a seemingly stable family life in Bombay (now Mumbai). Due to the nature of his service, Nanavati was frequently away, leaving Sylvia lonely. During one of his absences, Sylvia developed a relationship with Nanavati's friend, Prem Ahuja, a businessman. On April 27, 1959, Sylvia confessed to Nanavati about her affair, shocking him with the revelation that Ahuja was unlikely to marry her or take responsibility for their children. Consumed by betrayal, Nanavati drove to the naval base, collected a revolver, and headed to Ahuja's residence, determined to confront him.

When Nanavati reached Ahuja's apartment, he demanded that Ahuja marry Sylvia and take responsibility for their children.

Ahuja's refusal infuriated Nanavati, who then shot him dead. Following the killing, Nanavati turned himself in to the police, admitting to the crime but claiming he acted out of emotional turmoil. The murder was unprecedented in its media coverage and public interest, with Nanavati portrayed sympathetically by the public as a wronged husband.

## Facts of the Case

Key facts of the case included:

- Murder Weapon: Nanavati used a service revolver taken from the naval base to shoot Ahuja, which indicated premeditation, though he claimed it was in a moment of emotional turmoil.

- Witness Testimonies: Sylvia's confession, Nanavati's admission to the police, and physical evidence tied him directly to the murder.

- Public Sympathy and Media Influence: Due to the circumstances, Nanavati was seen by many as a victim of betrayal, resulting in widespread public support that significantly impacted the trial.

## Issues Raised

1. Premeditation or Emotional Impulse: The primary issue was whether Nanavati's act constituted premeditated murder or a crime committed in a state of temporary insanity.

2. Fair Trial: Given the overwhelming media coverage and public sentiment, the case raised concerns over the jury's impartiality, questioning the reliability of jury trials in high-profile cases.

## Laws Discussed

The legal discussion revolved around Section 302 of the Indian Penal Code, which defines murder, and Section 304, which allows for reduced charges in cases lacking intent or involving provocation. The case also highlighted provisions regarding the jury system, showing the necessity of impartiality in delivering justice.

## Arguments of the Parties

- Defense's Argument: Nanavati's defense argued that he acted out of a sudden and grave provocation after learning of his wife's affair. They claimed he was temporarily insane at the time of the killing, and his act was impulsive rather than premeditated. The defense sought a conviction under Section 304 for culpable homicide not amounting to murder, hoping for a lighter sentence.

- Prosecution's Argument: The prosecution argued that Nanavati's decision to retrieve a revolver from his naval base demonstrated intent and premeditation. They contended that Nanavati's actions were not those of a man in an uncontrollable rage but rather calculated revenge, warranting a murder conviction under Section 302.

## Judgment of the Case

The jury initially acquitted Nanavati by a majority of 8-1, reflecting the public sympathy he had garnered. However, the judge overseeing the trial disagreed with the jury's decision, sensing that it was biased due to media influence and public sentiment. He referred the case to the Bombay High Court under Section 307 of the Criminal Procedure Code, which allows a judge to overturn a jury verdict if they believe it to be legally flawed. The High Court found Nanavati guilty of murder, sentencing him to life imprisonment. This decision was later upheld by the Supreme Court, which agreed that the evidence supported a murder conviction rather than a lesser charge of culpable homicide.

## Analysis of the Judgment

The Nanavati judgment underscored the judiciary's role in ensuring impartiality, especially in cases swayed by public sentiment. The jury's acquittal, which appeared to be influenced by societal sympathies, highlighted the challenges of maintaining objectivity in a system where emotional biases could impact justice. The judge's intervention in the jury's decision illustrated the judiciary's responsibility to uphold the law impartially, regardless of public opinion. This case showcased the limitations of jury trials in India, where societal biases could potentially compromise justice in emotionally charged cases.

## Impact of the Judgment

The Nanavati case led to the abolition of the jury system in India in 1960. Recognizing the limitations of jury trials in high-profile cases, the Indian government concluded that complex and emotionally charged cases required trained judges who could interpret the law impartially without the influence of public opinion. This shift marked a significant transformation in India's legal system, ensuring that justice would be based on legal standards rather than societal biases.

Furthermore, the case highlighted the powerful role of the media in shaping public opinion and its potential impact on legal proceedings. The Nanavati case emphasized the need for responsible journalism, especially in cases where public emotions could influence the judicial process, reinforcing the importance of ethical reporting.

## Conclusion

The KM Nanavati vs. State of Maharashtra case remains a cornerstone of Indian legal history, marking the end of the jury system and solidifying the role of trained judges in delivering unbiased justice. This trial, with its intricate blend of personal betrayal, societal sympathy, and legal complexity, illustrated the need for a judicial system that prioritizes law over public sentiment. The Nanavati judgment has since served as a reminder of the judiciary's role in upholding the integrity of the legal process, ensuring that justice prevails even in the face of overwhelming public emotion.

*Scan Me to Download*

# CHAPTER-5

# VISHAKA VS. STATE OF RAJASTHAN: PIONEERING PROTECTIONS AGAINST WORKPLACE HARASSMENT

## Introduction

The Vishaka vs. State of Rajasthan case of 1997 is a landmark in India's judicial history that redefined workplace protections for women, especially against sexual harassment. This pivotal judgment, delivered by the Supreme Court of India, established what are now known as the Vishaka Guidelines, aimed at safeguarding women's dignity and ensuring gender equality in professional spaces. The case was catalyzed by the brutal gang rape of Bhanwari Devi, a social worker in Rajasthan, whose fight for justice exposed the absence of legal safeguards for women in workplaces. The Vishaka case stands as a testament to the power of judicial activism in creating laws where legislative gaps exist.

## Background of the Case

Bhanwari Devi, a lower-caste sathin (grassroots social worker) in Rajasthan, worked to prevent child marriages and promote women's welfare. In 1992, she attempted to stop a child marriage in her village, an act that provoked anger within the upper-caste community. As retribution, five men from the community gang-raped her while her husband was restrained. When Bhanwari Devi sought justice, she encountered severe resistance and systemic bias; the police hesitated to file a proper report, and medical professionals downplayed the assault in their documentation. Despite the trauma, Bhanwari continued her fight, eventually approaching the court.

The trial court acquitted all five accused men, citing a lack of evidence and suggesting that her husband's inability to prevent the assault cast doubt on her claims. This ruling incited outrage among women's rights organizations across the country, who saw the decision as emblematic of the deep-seated discrimination against women in the legal system. The Vishaka case thus began as a Public Interest Litigation (PIL) filed by Vishaka and several other NGOs, bringing attention to the widespread issue of workplace harassment and the urgent need for protective measures.

## Facts of the Case

Key facts in the Vishaka case included:

- The Assault: Bhanwari Devi was attacked by upper-caste men in retaliation for her social work, highlighting the intersecting challenges of caste, gender, and power dynamics.

- Judicial Bias: The initial trial court verdict demonstrated bias, failing to acknowledge the coercive conditions Bhanwari faced or to support her claims with due diligence.

- Legislative Gaps: India had no specific laws addressing workplace harassment at the time, leaving women vulnerable to such exploitation without any structured means of redress.

## Issues Raised

1. Gender Equality and Workplace Safety: The primary issue was the lack of legal protections for women facing harassment in workplaces.

2. Employer Responsibility: The case questioned whether employers should be legally obligated to prevent and address sexual harassment in the workplace.

3. Judicial Duty to Uphold Rights: In the absence of legislation, the Court faced the question of whether it could enact protective guidelines.

## Laws Discussed

The Supreme Court referenced fundamental rights enshrined in the Constitution of India:

- Article 14 (Right to Equality): Ensures equality before the law and protection from discrimination.

- Article 15 (Prohibition of Discrimination): Prohibits discrimination based on sex and empowers the state to make special provisions for women.

- Article 19(1)(g) (Right to Profession): Guarantees the right to practice any profession, implying that women have the right to a safe work environment.

- Article 21 (Right to Life and Dignity): Encompasses the right to live with dignity, extending to protection from harassment.

Additionally, the Court referred to international conventions, particularly the Convention on the Elimination of All Forms of Discrimination Against Women (CEDAW), to bolster the need for gender-sensitive workplace guidelines.

## Arguments of the Parties

- Petitioners' Argument: Representing Vishaka and other NGOs, the petitioners argued that the absence of workplace protections violated women's fundamental rights. They contended that without clear guidelines, women would continue to suffer harassment, thus deterring their full participation in the workforce. The petitioners urged the Court to adopt international standards as a stopgap measure until formal legislation was enacted.

- Respondent's Argument: The state of Rajasthan and central government argued that in the absence of specific laws on workplace harassment, they could not be held accountable. They contended that formulating workplace guidelines was the legislature's domain, not the judiciary's.

## Judgment of the Case

On August 13, 1997, the Supreme Court delivered a groundbreaking judgment. The Court ruled that, in the absence of legislation, it had the authority to establish guidelines for the prevention of sexual harassment at the workplace, citing its constitutional duty to uphold fundamental rights. Known as the Vishaka Guidelines, these directives required all workplaces to set up internal mechanisms to address complaints of harassment, including forming complaint committees with female members and representatives from women's NGOs.

The judgment defined sexual harassment broadly, encompassing physical advances, sexually colored remarks, and any unwelcome verbal or non-verbal behavior of a sexual nature. These guidelines, the Court asserted, would serve as the law until the legislature enacted specific regulations on workplace harassment. The decision placed the onus on employers to create a safe work environment, uphold dignity, and prevent gender-based discrimination.

## Analysis of the Judgment

The Vishaka judgment demonstrated the Court's proactive role in addressing urgent social issues in the absence of specific legislation. It underscored the judiciary's commitment to protecting women's rights and paved the way for safer workplaces. The Court's reliance on constitutional and international principles set a precedent, emphasizing that the lack of a domestic law should not hinder the enforcement of fundamental rights. However, the Court also indicated that these guidelines were an interim solution, placing the ultimate responsibility on the legislature to pass comprehensive workplace harassment laws.

## Impact of the Judgment

The Vishaka guidelines had an immediate and profound impact. They were implemented nationwide and significantly raised awareness about sexual harassment and women's rights in the workplace. This judgment served as the foundation for The Sexual Harassment of Women at Workplace (Prevention, Prohibition and Redressal) Act, which was passed in 2013. The Act codified the Vishaka Guidelines into a statutory framework, providing legal recourse for harassment victims and establishing structured grievance mechanisms.

By expanding the concept of workplace safety to include gender equality and personal dignity, the Vishaka case empowered countless women across India to pursue professional opportunities without fear of harassment. It underscored the responsibility of employers and institutions to foster a work environment that respects and upholds women's dignity.

## Conclusion

The Vishaka vs. State of Rajasthan case is a cornerstone of women's rights jurisprudence in India. It showcased the judiciary's power to safeguard fundamental rights by creating legal frameworks in the absence of existing laws. This judgment underscored the importance of a safe, dignified workplace for women, laying the groundwork for future reforms and influencing gender equality policies across various sectors. Today, the Vishaka

Guidelines symbolize a proactive approach to justice, reminding us that the law can and must evolve to protect the dignity and rights of every individual in society.

*Scan Me to Download*

# CHAPTER-6

# MARY ROY VS. STATE OF KERALA: A LANDMARK FOR WOMEN'S PROPERTY RIGHTS IN INDIA

## Introduction and Background of the Case

The Mary Roy vs. State of Kerala case, decided in 1986, marked a monumental turning point for women's rights in India, particularly regarding inheritance rights among the Christian community. This case arose from the challenge posed by Mary Roy, a Syrian Christian woman, against the outdated and discriminatory Travancore Christian Succession Act, 1092, which limited daughters' inheritance rights compared to sons. Mary Roy's courageous fight for equality highlighted the deep-seated gender bias in the existing laws and led to a Supreme Court ruling that established equal property rights for daughters, changing the inheritance landscape for Christian women in Kerala.

Mary Roy, the mother of renowned author Arundhati Roy, was left without a fair share of her father's property after his passing. She discovered that, according to the Travancore Christian Succession Act, daughters received only a limited share of the family estate, while sons inherited the lion's share. This law, rooted in patriarchal norms, denied women the right to inherit family property on equal terms with men. Determined to challenge this, Mary Roy filed a petition, asserting her right to equality under the Indian Constitution.

## Facts of the Case

Key facts of the case include:

- Discriminatory Succession Law: Under the Travancore Christian Succession Act, daughters received only a fraction of the inheritance compared to sons. This law restricted daughters to a life interest, while sons gained full ownership.

- Personal Impact on Mary Roy: Mary Roy was denied an equal share of her father's estate, an injustice that reflected broader issues of gender discrimination in inheritance rights.

- Legal Challenge: Roy's petition questioned the constitutionality of the Travancore Christian Succession Act, arguing that it violated her fundamental right to equality under Article 14 of the Indian Constitution.

## Issues Raised

The Mary Roy case raised fundamental issues, including:

1. Equality in Inheritance Rights: Did the Travancore Christian Succession Act violate the right to equality by granting unequal inheritance rights based on gender?

2. Applicability of the Indian Succession Act: Could the Indian Succession Act of 1925, which provides equal inheritance rights, override the discriminatory provisions of the Travancore Christian Succession Act?

3. Legal Reforms for Women's Rights: Did this case warrant a broader judicial push for uniform succession laws across India to protect women's rights?

## Laws Discussed

The legal framework addressed in this case involved:

- Article 14 of the Indian Constitution: This article guarantees the right to equality, which Mary Roy argued was violated by the unequal inheritance provisions of the Travancore Christian Succession Act.

- Indian Succession Act, 1925: The Supreme Court examined whether the Indian Succession Act, which provided equal rights for male and female heirs, should govern Christian inheritance laws in Kerala.

- Travancore Christian Succession Act, 1092: This law, specific to Christians in Travancore, discriminated against daughters in property inheritance and formed the basis of Roy's legal challenge.

## Arguments of the Parties

- Petitioner's Argument (Mary Roy):

  - Roy argued that the Travancore Christian Succession Act's discriminatory provisions violated her fundamental right to equality under Article 14. She asserted that the Indian Succession Act, 1925, which had been extended to Part B states (including Travancore), should govern inheritance for Christians in Kerala.

  - She argued that Christian women, like herself, should not be denied the same rights afforded to men and called for the application of the Indian Succession Act to provide equal inheritance rights.

- Respondent's Argument (State of Kerala):

- The State argued that the Travancore Christian Succession Act was specific to the region and had not been superseded by the Indian Succession Act.

- The respondents contended that the discriminatory provisions in the law were protected by religious practices and did not warrant intervention.

## Judgment of the Case

In a landmark ruling, the Supreme Court of India struck down the Travancore Christian Succession Act, declaring that the Indian Succession Act, 1925, would govern the inheritance rights of Christians in Kerala. The Court held that the outdated Travancore law was repealed by the Part B States (Laws) Act, 1951, which extended the Indian Succession Act to the region. This decision granted Christian women in Kerala the same inheritance rights as their male relatives, aligning the region's inheritance laws with the constitutional guarantee of equality under Article 14.

The Court emphasized that discriminatory laws based on gender or religion must yield to the principles of justice, equality, and fairness, as enshrined in the Indian Constitution.

## Analysis of the Judgment

This judgment underscored the judiciary's role in advancing gender justice by ensuring equality before the law. The ruling clarified that regional laws conflicting with fundamental rights must be set aside. The Court's decision signified a bold judicial stance in favor of women's rights, establishing a precedent for challenging other discriminatory personal laws across religious communities. This judgment also highlighted the importance of a uniform legal framework for succession that respects both religious diversity and individual rights.

## Impact of the Judgment

The Mary Roy judgment had profound implications for Indian law and society:

1. Equal Inheritance Rights for Christian Women: The decision granted Christian women in Kerala inheritance rights equal to men, transforming the financial autonomy and empowerment of countless women.

2. Precedent for Gender Equality in Personal Laws: This case inspired advocacy for reforms in other religious personal laws, encouraging movements toward uniform and equitable succession laws across communities.

3. Progressive Judicial Activism: The judgment reflected the judiciary's commitment to upholding fundamental rights and eliminating gender-based discrimination, setting a model for future legal reforms supporting women's rights.

## Conclusion

The Mary Roy vs. State of Kerala case is a landmark in India's journey toward gender equality, particularly within the realm of inheritance rights. Mary Roy's tenacity in challenging discriminatory laws inspired a judicial shift, affirming that no woman should be denied her rightful inheritance due to her gender. This case redefined legal standards for Christian inheritance in Kerala, catalyzed movements for reform across other communities, and reinforced the role of the judiciary in safeguarding equality and justice. Today, the Mary Roy judgment stands as a testament to the power of individual courage in dismantling entrenched biases, creating a lasting impact on Indian law and society.

*Scan Me to Download*

CHAPTER-7

# R. RAJAGOPAL (AUTO SHANKAR) VS. STATE OF TAMIL NADU: PRIVACY VS. PRESS FREEDOM IN INDIA

## Introduction and Background of the Case

The R. Rajagopal vs. State of Tamil Nadu case, also known as the "Auto Shankar Case," marks a defining moment in Indian jurisprudence at the intersection of privacy rights and freedom of the press. Decided on October 7, 1994, this case centered on the publication of an autobiography written by Gauri Shankar (alias Auto Shankar), a convicted serial killer on death row, who documented his criminal connections with certain state officials. The revelations threatened to expose illegal activities among high-ranking officials, and the state sought to block its publication on grounds of defamation and privacy. This case compelled the judiciary to confront the complexities of press freedom, privacy, and accountability, setting a landmark precedent on these issues.

## Facts of the Case

1. The Autobiography: Auto Shankar, a notorious criminal convicted of multiple murders, allegedly penned an autobiography while incarcerated, revealing connections with various government officials who facilitated his illegal activities. He reportedly handed the manuscript to his wife with instructions to deliver it to his advocate for eventual publication.

2. State Intervention: Upon learning of the impending publication, prison officials allegedly pressured Shankar to withdraw consent. They threatened legal action against the publisher, claiming that the publication contained defamatory content that could harm the reputations of public servants.

3. Legal Petition: The magazine Nakkheeran, which planned to publish the autobiography, filed a writ petition in the Supreme Court under Article 32 of the Indian Constitution. The petitioners argued that the state's attempt to block publication violated freedom of the press under Article 19(1)(a).

## Issues Raised

The case raised fundamental questions regarding:

1. Privacy and Freedom of Expression: Can an individual prevent unauthorized publication of their biography on privacy grounds? Is freedom of expression an absolute right?

2. Defamation and Prior Restraint: Can the state impose prior restraint on the press to prevent potential defamation?

3. Rights of Prisoners: Are prison officials justified in preventing a prisoner's autobiography from being published to protect the individual's privacy?

## Laws Discussed

The Supreme Court's decision examined the following constitutional and legal provisions:

- Article 19(1)(a): Grants freedom of speech and expression to Indian citizens, including the press's right to publish matters of public interest.

- Article 21: Ensures the right to life and personal liberty, interpreted to include the right to privacy.

- Sections 499 and 500 of the IPC: Define defamation and its punishments, forming the legal basis for restrictions on harmful speech.

## Arguments of the Parties

- Petitioners (Nakkheeran and Editor):

  - Argued that they had a constitutional right to publish the autobiography under Article 19(1)(a), especially as it disclosed criminal activities involving public officials.

  - Claimed the state could not exercise prior restraint solely on grounds of potential defamation and that Auto Shankar's criminal connections were of significant public interest.

- Respondents (State of Tamil Nadu):

  - Argued that the publication could tarnish reputations and jeopardize the privacy rights of involved officials.

  - Claimed the autobiography's authenticity was questionable, as Shankar allegedly denied authorizing its publication.

## Judgment of the Case

In a landmark judgment, the Supreme Court ruled in favor of the petitioners, affirming the right of the press to publish Shankar's autobiography. The Court's key findings included:

1. Privacy Rights: The Court recognized that privacy is intrinsic to personal liberty under Article 21. However, this right does not extend to shield illegal activities, especially when they involve public officials.

2. Public Interest and Prior Restraint: The state cannot impose prior restraint based on concerns of defamation. Any defamation claims must be pursued post-publication, and the press must be allowed to function freely to ensure public accountability.

3. Prisoner's Rights: While prisoners have privacy rights, these do not justify preemptive censorship, particularly when the publication concerns matters of public record.

The Court thus allowed Nakkheeran to publish the autobiography's content, affirming that privacy claims do not override freedom of expression in cases where public interest is at stake.

### Analysis of the Judgment

The Court's decision balanced privacy with the press's essential role in exposing misconduct. The ruling emphasized that privacy rights do not provide immunity from scrutiny in cases where public officials may be involved in criminal activities. However, the Court specified that unauthorized publication of personal details (unrelated to public record) would still constitute an invasion of privacy. This judgment reinforced that only post-publication remedies, such as defamation suits, are permissible, thereby limiting state power to impose prior restraint on the press.

## Impact of the Judgment

The R. Rajagopal case had profound and far-reaching impacts on Indian law:

1. Strengthened Press Freedom: This decision established a strong precedent for press freedom, allowing the media to publish content in the public interest without fear of preemptive censorship.

2. Reinforced Privacy Rights: While endorsing press freedom, the judgment affirmed privacy as a fundamental right, laying groundwork for its recognition in future cases, notably in the Puttaswamy v. Union of India ruling in 2017.

3. Curb on State Interference: By limiting the state's ability to impose prior restraint, the ruling underscored that public accountability cannot be overridden by the state's interests in protecting reputations.

## Conclusion

The R. Rajagopal vs. State of Tamil Nadu case remains a cornerstone of Indian legal history, underscoring the balance between privacy and freedom of expression. This judgment established that while individuals have a right to privacy, this right is not absolute, especially when public interest is at stake. The Court reinforced the media's crucial role in democratic society, limiting the state's power to suppress information preemptively. The decision echoes today as a testament to India's commitment to transparency, accountability, and individual freedoms within a constitutional framework.

*Scan Me to Download*

# CONCLUSION

As we close the pages of 7 Landmark Cases That Changed the Indian Judicial System, we're reminded of the power of the judiciary to transform society, one ruling at a time. Each case explored in this book has left an indelible mark on India's legal landscape, bringing clarity, reform, and justice where ambiguity, inequality, and injustices once prevailed. These landmark judgments demonstrate how the law, when wielded with integrity, can serve as a force for profound change, ensuring that justice remains the bedrock of a fair society.

From the harrowing Nirbhaya case that overhauled India's approach to sexual violence, to Mary Roy's tireless fight for equal inheritance rights, each chapter in this book highlights not only the courage of the individuals involved but also the judiciary's commitment to upholding the values enshrined in our Constitution. These cases underscore that the legal system is more than a collection of rules—it's a living entity, evolving to meet the needs of its citizens and to protect the values of equality, liberty, and dignity.

Through these decisions, we see the judiciary's role in balancing rights and responsibilities, whether addressing the boundaries of privacy and free speech, challenging archaic personal laws, or reinforcing the rights of the most vulnerable in society. Each case, in its own way, reminds us that the judiciary is often the last refuge for those seeking justice and equality.

While much has been achieved, these cases also serve as a reminder that the journey is ongoing. India's legal system must continue to adapt to new challenges, from digital privacy concerns and evolving social norms to the global human rights discourse. The judiciary's role in addressing these issues will shape the future of Indian democracy, as it has in the past.

7 Landmark Cases That Changed the Indian Judicial System is more than a look at case law; it is a celebration of India's commitment to justice. May it inspire us to appreciate, defend, and strengthen the rule of law, for only through a just and fair judiciary can society truly thrive.